W9-BVA-054

GOD AND THE
WELFARE STATE

GOD AND THE WELFARE STATE

Lew Daly

Foreword by James Carroll

BOSTON REVIEW Somerville, Mass.

THE MIT PRESS Cambridge, Mass. London, England

MIT Press books may be purchased at special quantity discounts for business or sales promotional use. For information, please e-mail special_sales@mitpress.mit.edu or write to Special Sales Department, The MIT Press, 55 Hayward Street, Cambridge, MA 02142.

This book was set in Adobe Garamond by *Boston Review* and was printed and bound in the United States of America.

Designed by Joshua J. Friedman

Library of Congress Cataloging-in-Publication Data
Daly, Lew.
  God and the welfare state / Lew Daly.
    p.   cm. — (Boston Review books)
  Includes bibliographical references (p.   ).
  ISBN-13: 978-0-262-04236-9 (alk. paper)
  ISBN-10: 0-262-04236-3 (alk. paper)
  1. Poverty—Religious aspects—Christianity. 2. Church work with the poor—United States. 3. Faith-based human services. 4. Church and social problems—United States.
5. United States—Economic conditions. 6. United States—Social conditions. I. Title.
BV4647.P6D35 2006
361.7′50973—dc22   2006049436

10 9 8 7 6 5 4 3 2 1

For Pam, Bev, and Anne—
I will fear no evil, for you are with me

America, you must be born again.

MARTIN LUTHER KING JR.

CONTENTS

James Carroll

FOREWORD

THE DISASTER ON THE GULF COAST IN
September 2005 was an occasion for public
prayer. President Bush invited the nation
to place the victims of Hurricane Katrina
in the hands of an all-loving God, an im-
pulse many of us shared. In many cities,
religious figures were at the forefront of wel-
come expressions of concern. On the scene
of the catastrophe itself, religious organizations provided heroic relief, often in stark
contrast to hesitant government agencies.
The value—and values—of religion were
on full display.

And yet Katrina's aftermath opened a curtain on the new and troublesome place religion occupies in American culture. I found myself wondering if the abysmal performance of government agencies in responding to this crisis wasn't related to the unprecedented emphasis the government has been putting on "faith-based" groups as key providers of social services. There is nothing new, of course, in religious organizations as generous suppliers of various public needs. One thinks of the parochial-school system and the Salvation Army. But politicians in Washington and the state capitals have exploited this tradition of religious generosity to justify the rollback of programs dating to the New Deal.

Why is the shift from government to religion troubling? Doesn't it square with the idea that common-good activities flourish from the grass roots up? And isn't religion essentially a matter of compassionate love, an ideal no one would claim for public institutions? Religion directly addresses the mystery of death and suffering: what better institution to meet the needs of those who suffer? And aren't religiously motivated providers, for whom the cardinal virtues are professional qualifications, less prone to corruptions large and small? What's to choose between, say, Mother Teresa and a form-obsessed social worker? Wouldn't we all prefer to have our needs met by the communion of the saints?

These are the difficult questions that Lew Daly grapples with admirably in *God and the Welfare State*, which engages the Christian ideas behind the faith-based initiative. Daly takes these ideas very seriously, since they go to the heart of the relationship between religion, government, and social welfare and underlie the low poverty rates of Europe's Christian Democracies.

Daly sees hope in these ideas but also finds that, as they have taken shape in the Bush administration, they represent a truly radical departure from both Christian European and secular American models. Religiously sponsored good works are replacing public responsibility, and something essential to democracy is at stake. The rights of citizens to basic relief, especially in times of crisis, are in fact based not in charity but in another religious idea: justice.

"Faith-based" substitutes for the provision of basic needs to the poor disguise a hidden agenda. The destruction of public social services has been nothing less than an attack on people in need, as if their need itself is deserving of punishment. The war on poverty has become a war on the poor. That it is waged in the name of God, in alliance with those who claim to honor God, is blasphemy.

PREFACE

IN THE MID-1990S I LEFT ACADEMIA TO enter the ministry. This decision came out of my experience at a small urban church in Buffalo, New York, where both of my children were baptized and of which my wife and children and I remain members to this day. My pastor in Buffalo had gone to Union Theological Seminary in New York City, and, as is fairly common in parish life, I followed in his footsteps.

The time I spent in seminary, 1996 through 1999, coincided with what is perhaps the greatest abuse of religious authority since the rise of America's vaunted "religious right": the Clinton impeachment crisis, which some commentators described as an attempted theocratic coup d'état, diverted me from my path to ordination. I never completed the theological paper I needed to write. Although the requirement in itself was relatively uncomplicated—I had already written a doctoral dissertation—my mind was elsewhere, and I despaired of becoming a pastor.

I had seen the power of religious healing, unforgettably, when I did pastoral work in a federal prison. But the broader public life of American religion had become something alien to that power. Like the criminal-justice system itself, American religion had become a disease of the state, something that was destroying the country from within. I took solace in the Bible's teachings about false religion and failed states. To be sure, the culture war's preachers and potentates are a classic lot. They are playing their parts in the Bible story—the parts of royal priests and false prophets who violate God's justice while acting in God's name.

Something else in my experience sharpens the feeling that perhaps we are entering a transformative, prophetic time. Since leaving home in rural upstate New York, I have lived almost exclusively in poor urban neighborhoods while also being connected to elite institutions. The juxtaposition of rich and poor has made me see those different worlds as an integrated system of oppression.

Poverty in the midst of plenty is the most basic moral reality any advanced nation must confront, but in the United States it is more than that. Here, poverty amid plenty is a political way of life. And disturbingly, the apparent "desecularization" of recent decades (as some scholars are now calling it) seems only to have ingrained this contradiction more deeply: in no other country would shrinking the welfare rolls by more than half while millions fall into poverty be defined as a policy success by all the major political parties.

It may be puzzling that, despite all this, I find the confessional ideas and history behind the faith-based initiative—the subject of this book—worth studying and perhaps even applying (if one could do so more truthfully and consistently than President Bush has done—exactly how will be clearer when you finish reading, I hope). At a minimum the political theology of the faith-based initiative—as the thinking involved here should be described—is truly innovative. It takes us beyond the culture war and the entrenched church–state positions of the day, which have never contributed anything to the struggle against poverty.

GOD AND THE
WELFARE STATE

1

AMERICA'S EXCEPTIONAL RELIGIOSITY is actually less exceptional, among advanced countries, than its record of failure on poverty and inequality. If this is God's "chosen nation," it is not as Isaiah promised—a place where the people will benefit from their own labors; where they will no longer "build houses for others to live in" or "plant for others to eat"; where they will not "toil in vain or bear children doomed to misfortune."

God seems to have a clear policy on poverty. And President George W. Bush believes that in restricting support for religious groups that care for those in need, the government discriminates against God's work and creates the largest barrier to reducing poverty today. Thus, he has made it a priority of his administration to secure a larger share of federal social-welfare resources for religious groups, an effort he describes as being inspired by the Hebrew prophets and as the missing link in the war on poverty. It is his signature policy—perhaps the one thing he has done as president that he truly believes in.

The Faith-Based and Community Initiative, as it is officially called, has been a source of controversy throughout Bush's two terms. Many have focused their criticism on the program's constitutionality. This is a losing battle, and for those who take the fight against poverty seriously it is also the wrong battle. The constitutionality of federal aid to religious social-service providers is becoming increasingly plausible as the structure and purpose of the welfare state evolves.

Other critics have focused, more cynically, on the threat of political patronage and vote-buying in poor communities. One near caricature of this problem is the Reverend Herbert Lusk of North Philadelphia's Greater Exodus Baptist Church. Lusk endorsed Bush during the 2000 Republican National Convention via satellite from his church, and in 2002 his church's social-service arm received a million-dollar grant from the U.S. Administration for Children and Families. Another influential Philadelphia pastor, Luis Cortes, says that although he voted for Ralph Nader in 2000, he shifted allegiances in 2004 after his community-development corporation,

Nueva Esperanza, received a $7.2 million grant from the faith-based initiative in 2003. So far, however, these endorsements from prominent pastors have not done much for the Republicans in Philadelphia.

Still other critics have argued, rightly, that there is little scientific evidence that social services provided by religious organizations are more effective than those of conventional nonprofits, let alone so effective as to warrant a major government initiative. Many people simply assume they are more effective, sometimes because this is what they hear in the media but often because they have seen some successes in their own church or neighborhood. The religious aspects of these programs certainly benefit some people. But as a legislative and social matter, the "faith factor" is today, at best, only a testable hypothesis. John DiIulio, the

6

first director of the White House Office of Faith-Based and Community Initiatives and the most prominent social scientist among the program's supporters, wrote in 2002, "We do not yet know … whether America's religious armies of compassion, local or national, large or small, measurably outperform their secular counterparts."

These critics raise legitimate concerns. But they must concede that the faith-based initiative is no threat to some great achievements of the past: since Lyndon Johnson's War on Poverty in the mid-1960s the poverty rate has remained essentially unchanged, under Democrats and Republicans alike. If the architects of the faith-based initiative claim that it will effectively fight poverty, skeptics and believers both would do well to consider it on its own terms before passing judgment.

A product of serious thinkers with precise theological convictions, the faith-based initiative draws on doctrines that first emerged in European Christianity's conflict with liberalism and socialism in the late 19th century. Rooted in Calvinism and Catholicism, these doctrines assign a public purpose to religious organizations and ordain government to help those organizations fulfill that purpose without interference. Together they constitute a distinctive religious theory of the limited state, the goal of which is not to privatize welfare but to shift public authority to self-governing religious groups.

To judge the faith-based initiative we need to understand the convictions of its designers and its likely consequences. The consequences matter, and for those whose principal concern is fighting poverty and who are prepared to consider new means for conducting that fight, government support for religious groups may be attractive at first glance.

This book ultimately asks whether policies claiming religious inspiration are faithful to the teachings they invoke. It is also a book about the influence of ideas in policymaking—the intellectual genealogy of a major political change. Indeed, for anyone seeking to understand why philosophy matters in contemporary politics, there is no better case study than the faith-based initiative. For the first time, core theological principles of the Christian tradition have been systematically applied to federal administration and spending. "We don't just talk about abortion or other specific issues," one prominent advocate, James Skillen, explains. "We want to ask about the nature of government."

If there is hope in the faith-based initiative, it lies not in the program itself but in the ideas that guide it. Through a theological lens we can appreciate the deeper political significance of the faith-based initiative and understand how it betrays its founding ideas and ignores disturbing dimensions of their past. And this opens the door to a valuable debate on government, religion, and poverty that neither opponents nor proponents of religious involvement in public life are prepared to have.

2

As Ronald Reagan had done before him, George W. Bush delivered his first commencement address as president at the University of Notre Dame, the nation's leading Catholic intellectual center. Back in 1981, Reagan had given a folksy reminiscence of the Notre Dame football legend George Gipp, whom he had portrayed in the 1940 film *Knute Rockne—All American*. The students could "win one for the Gipper," Reagan essentially said, by going out and defending the private sector from government interference and usurpations. He added a brief reference to the recent assassination attempt on Pope John Paul II, suggesting that it had something to do with "certain economic theories that use the rhetoric of class struggle to justify injustice."

Twenty years later, on May 20, 2001, President Bush delivered a very different speech. Instead of a war on government, he urged a "determined assault" on poverty. The policy successes of Lyndon Johnson's War on Poverty, such as Medicaid, were just the first phase of a much longer war, Bush argued. The second phase was Clinton-era welfare reform, which "confronted welfare dependency." Now, a third phase was needed to complete the job. Government still has a place, he said, but now it must "take the side of charities and community healers." There was no more hiding from the fact that "any effective war on poverty must deploy what Dorothy Day called 'the weapons of the spirit.'" In this work, Bush said, the "Jewish prophets and Catholic teaching" can guide us with their insistence on God's special concern for the poor, "perhaps the most radical teaching of faith":

> When poverty is considered hopeless, America is condemned to permanent social division, becoming a nation of caste and class, divided by fences and gates and guards.
>
> Our task is clear, and it's difficult: we must build our country's unity by extending our country's blessings. We make that commitment because we are Americans. Aspiration is the essence of our country. We believe in social mobility, not social Darwinism. We are the country of the second chance, where failure is never final. And that dream has sometimes been deferred. It must never be abandoned.

We are committed to compassion for practical reasons. When men and women are lost to themselves, they are also lost to our nation. When millions are hopeless, all of us are diminished by the loss of their gifts.

Memorable words from a more promising time in his presidency, perhaps. But not only that. George W. Bush had been promoting the provision of welfare by religious groups, mainly through executive powers, since 1995, the first year of his first term as Texas governor. Something genuinely new was happening when Bush came to the aid of religious social-service providers in Texas: the basic ideas behind the faith-based initiative were being set into motion.

In the spring of 1995 the Texas Commission on Alcohol and Drug Abuse threatened to suspend the license of the San Antonio branch of a religious substance-abuse treatment organization called Teen Challenge. Founded in 1958, Teen Challenge has over 150 centers in the United States and 250 worldwide; its stated mission is to "evangelize people who have life-controlling problems and initiate the discipleship process." According to a report in *The New York Times Magazine*, Jim Heurich, the head of the San Antonio branch, "sums up the secret of his success in two words: Jesus Christ."

Teen Challenge refused to comply with the state's demands (which included the licensing of its counselors) and became a national martyr. In the summer of 1995, the National Center for Neighborhood Enterprise sponsored a demonstration on its behalf at the Alamo. Marvin Olasky, a Texas journalism professor and the editor of a Christian magazine, published a now famous op-ed in *The Wall Street Journal* attacking government regulation of religious social-service providers. Clint Bolick's Institute for Justice, known for its litigation in support of school-voucher programs, mounted a legal challenge and orchestrated news coverage on NBC. And George W. Bush intervened to stop the state commission from revoking Teen Challenge's license.

That fall the Institute for Justice negotiated an out-of-court victory for Teen Challenge through a consent order allowing it to practice without a license. And the following spring Bush issued the first of many executive orders devoted to helping religious social-service providers. In it he established the Governor's Advisory Task Force on Faith-Based Community Service Groups, with the mandate of determining "how Texas can best create an environment in which these organizations can flourish and most effectively help those in need."

In December 1996 the task force released its report, *Faith in Action: A New Vision for Church–State Cooperation in Texas*. Compiled with the guidance of Marvin Olasky, the Christian social-policy scholar Stanley Carlson-Thies, and the constitutional scholar Carl Esbeck (the latter two would assume senior positions in the White House), it offered a blueprint for enlarging the public role of religious social-service providers:

> We must move beyond "devolution"— merely parsing duties between different levels of government—and embrace genuine reform that sparks cooperation between government (at whatever level) and the institutions of civil society. We must think anew about the relationship between government and non-government, and,

ultimately, vest power *beyond* government back to individuals and social institutions. We must offer a vision of rebuilding—and remoralizing—distressed communities, not through government, but through the ideals and civilizing institutions that nurture lives and transmit values.

Faith in Action outlines the radical core of Bush's policy vision. Several themes stand out today: its emphasis on religious ministries' "inner conversion" as a starting point for effective social services; its interpretation of the "charitable choice" provision of the 1996 federal welfare-reform bill as something that "invites the privatization of welfare through private and religious charities"; its frontal attack on state licensure and regulation in child-care and addiction-treatment services; and its quest to overtake even the devolution of responsibility for so-cial welfare from the federal government to the states.

In 1997 the Texas legislature carried out the task force's recommendations by pass-ing three bills to ease or eliminate legal and regulatory barriers affecting religious social-service providers. Bush also issued an execu-tive order requiring state agencies to take "affirmative steps," as prescribed by federal law, "to protect the religious integrity and the functional autonomy of participating faith-based providers."

The evidence from Texas reveals the faith-based initiative's particular view of government: it has helped to "undermine civil society" with public welfare programs, and now it must "replenish and enable" re-ligious organizations and "coax and nurture these institutions back to health."

3

IN 1996, THE WASHINGTON TIMES
published an article under the headline
"100-year-old idea inspires proposal to re-
vamp welfare." The article connected present-day thinking on welfare reform to the
theories of the Dutch statesman and theo-
logian Abraham Kuyper. Michael Gerson,
then a speechwriter and policy director for
Senator Dan Coats (R-Ind.), is quoted as
saying that the Kuyperian influence "has
the makings of a movement."

A small but dedicated network of religious intellectuals had set out to reverse

the secularizing influence that government contracts were said to be having on religious social-service providers. By the late 1990s they had galvanized a small circle of legislators called the Renewal Alliance.

In a 1997 lecture Coats described the project as being "consistent with a great and noble tradition of Catholic and Protestant social thought originating before the turn of the century with Pope Leo XIII and Abraham Kuyper." Two core ideas, said Coats, the Catholic doctrine of subsidiarity and the Dutch Calvinist theory of sphere sovereignty, "have enriched our political debates with some basic principles." But the Renewal Alliance made little headway, and by the time Coats retired from the Senate in 1999, a new, more powerful champion of these ideas was on his way to the White House, executive blueprint in hand.

Subsidiarity and sphere sovereignty emerged in the late 19th century, when socialist movements and the rise of liberal welfare states in Europe threatened religious power in key social domains including education and welfare. Both doctrines assert self-rule for religious organizations within the liberal state and require government to help them fulfill their public purposes without interference.

Historically, these doctrines played a formative role in the development of European Christian Democracy. With the defeat of fascism after the Second World War, Christian Democratic parties came to power in many parts of Europe. The subsidiary welfare model they implemented rejected the strong central state of socialism on the one hand and the unbridled free markets of capitalism on the other. With generous social-welfare provisions, Christian Democracy sought a compromise between social democracy's economic interventionism and Anglo-American welfare systems, which typically tied health, retirement, and other benefits to employment and left the needs of the unemployed to a public welfare system. Christian Democratic states featured limited state control of social services yet social-spending levels roughly as high as in social-democratic systems, and even higher in some cases.

Interestingly, by the 1970s, countries with a strong Christian Democratic presence were among the most secularized in the world. But the United States suffered no comparable decline in religious adherence or participation. If anything, the evidence suggests that the United States was becoming desecularized, particularly in political life.

It was in the 1980s that a small group of American religious conservatives with Christian Democratic roots first began to explore ways to integrate key ideas from their tradition into social policy. This effort operated at some distance from the main currents of conservative religious activism, which were then dominated by efforts to stop abortion and protect school prayer.

The debate over welfare reform in the mid-1990s gave momentum to a more sophisticated, institutional approach. Small think tanks such as the Center for Public Justice, with Dutch Calvinist roots, and the Acton Institute, with social-Catholic roots, gained influence by adding religious dimensions to the debate. Their efforts reached a turning point when the 1996 welfare-reform bill passed, and with it a provision for "charitable choice."

Introduced to little fanfare by then-senator John Ashcroft, charitable choice essentially gave religious social-service providers a statutory right to contract with the government without sacrificing their religious character. Since the 1996 welfare-reform bill, three other major laws and at least eight other bills introduced in Congress have incorporated charitable-choice provisions. As of 2001, charitable choice applied to programs disseminating nearly $22 billion in federal funds annually.

The most controversial aspect of charitable choice is that it allows churches to discriminate on the basis of religion in hiring for federally funded programs: it permits, for example, a Baptist church that runs a government-funded homeless shelter to hire only Baptists. This issue derailed any further legislative expansion of charitable choice during Bush's first term. But it began working its way through the courts in 2005, and on September 30 a U.S. district-court judge in New York issued a momentous ruling. In *Lown v. Salvation Army*, Judge Sidney Stein essentially found that government funding does not automatically trigger constitutional restrictions on religious entities' hiring practices, though legislatures may make such restrictions a condition of receiving public funds.

There is a degree of common sense in this: it does, in fact, seem discriminatory to force religious organizations to hire people who don't share their beliefs. An analogous secular contractor might be Planned Parenthood, which receives substantial funding from the federal government. Planned Parenthood operates according to strong principles of reproductive choice. Yet it is not obligated to hire people who reject those principles for programs that receive federal funds.

The *Lown* ruling reflects a broader trend. Since the late 1980s the Supreme Court has steadily moved in the direction of allowing federal funding of, or in-kind support for, public services provided by religious institutions, primarily in education and social welfare. Building on a theory of neutrality between religious and non-religious providers of public services, this trend began with the 1988 landmark ruling in *Bowen v. Kendrick*. *Bowen* upheld the constitutionality of the Adolescent Family Life Act, which authorized the government to fund religious providers of sex education. The ruling established a presumption of constitutionality for such arrangements, contingent on formal neutrality between different religions and between religion and non-religion, as well as clear secular purpose in the services provided. From then on a challenge would require proof that federal funds were being used for inherently religious purposes.

Neutrality theory bodes well for highly religious providers in direct-aid cases, according to some experts. Carl Esbeck argues that if the Supreme Court continues to expand its application of neutrality theory in material-aid cases, this is likely to take the form of "permitting direct funding of what now would be considered pervasively sectarian social-service organizations."

And if it becomes clear that the social services delivered by religious organizations are more effective—as John DiIulio and others are devoting themselves to proving—it is highly unlikely that the current boundaries will stand. If people are persuaded that religion is truly making a difference in troubled lives, abstract constitutional doctrines barring government aid will seem less and less compelling—except, perhaps, in situations where some religions are being favored over others.

The Supreme Court's new trajectory is partly motivated, in other words, by the highly experimental political environment that gave rise to welfare reform and the faith-based initiative. No principled defense of the Establishment Clause, whatever its theoretical validity, is likely to slow these changes.

4

THE EFFECT OF THE "FAITH FACTOR" on Bush's presidency has been treated widely and at length, mainly as a personal trait. But the primary influence of Christian Democratic ideas has gone virtually unnoticed. One reason is simply that Christian Democracy is little understood in the United States. Another is that the faith-based initiative's administrative form has been unfolding outside the legislative spotlight.

The White House did not necessarily want new legislation introduced when it launched the faith-based initiative. Existing charitable-choice law provided the basic authority it needed to carry out the president's plan through executive action. In fact, the administrative focus of the faith-based initiative reveals a striking consistency with the religious ideas at its origins. Subsidiarity and sphere sovereignty are doctrines of governance, requiring comprehensive administrative and regulatory attention of a sort that cuts across particular programs and laws.

To some, the faith-based initiative may look like mere cover for the old laissez-faire agenda of dismantling public programs. But it is not simply a bid to replace public welfare with religious charity, or to leave individuals alone, stranded in the market, as the writer Barbara Ehrenreich and others have argued. Rather, it is an effort to hollow out the welfare state by relinquishing its public authority to religious groups. As

Coats put it at a 1996 Heritage Foundation symposium, there is a need to "creatively surrender federal authority to civil society" and encourage a "transfer of resources and authority … to those private and religious institutions that shape, direct, and reclaim individual lives." The result could be well financed or poorly financed, but the essential feature of the new system is the transfer of control over services, and even policy, to religious groups.

These groups are treated by the initiative as self-governing entities, ordained by God to foster a well-balanced social order, operating through public power but not under it. The state, by transferring resources to these groups while relinquishing powers of governance over them, fulfills *its* ordained role as a support system that enables religion do its work.

Although no additional laws were needed to create the faith-based initiative, Bush has enacted a series of structural and administrative changes that have been virtually invisible to the public but that have had far-reaching effects.

Shortly after he took office, Bush issued two executive orders to launch the faith-based initiative. The first created the White House Office of Faith-Based and Community Initiatives. The second created satellite offices in each of the five major domestic cabinet agencies—Health and Human Services, Housing and Urban Development, Labor, Education, and Justice. This alone was a major innovation in presidential history: creating an infrastructure for helping churches collaborate with the government. The satellite offices were then ordered to conduct in-depth audits of rules, regulations, procurement practices, and outreach methods in each department with the goal of removing barriers to religious social-service providers. In the summer of 2001, the White House issued *Unlevel Playing Field*, a report synthesizing the findings of the audits. Although similar in inspiration to the report of Bush's Texas task force, *Faith in Action*, the new report was more guarded, trading language about welfare "undermining civil society" for arguments about the need to end government "bias" against religious groups. It became the technical road map for putting the faith-based initiative into action throughout the government.

More executive orders followed in December 2002 and June 2004, establishing satellite offices in the Departments of Agriculture, Commerce, and Veterans Affairs; in the Agency for International Development;

and in the Small Business Administration. Another executive order, issued in December 2002, established "equal protection of the laws for faith-based and community organizations." Charitable-choice principles were essentially being extended to all federally financed social-service programs.

The nonpartisan Roundtable on Religion and Social Welfare Policy, based at SUNY Albany and financed by the Pew Charitable Trusts, analyzes this effort in a 2004 report called *The Expanding Administrative Presidency*. "In the absence of new legislative authority," the report says, "the President has aggressively advanced the Faith-Based Initiative through executive orders, rule changes, managerial realignment in federal agencies, and other innovative uses of the prerogatives of his office." Other presidents, from FDR to Ronald Reagan, have used executive powers in similar ways, but these efforts "typically lack *local cells* that provide the *feet and hands* needed to organize and implement presidential initiatives." What Bush has done differently is to endow his initiative with a coordinated transgovernmental infrastructure. Overseen from the White House, the satellite offices are "empowered to articulate, advance and oversee *coordinated* efforts to win more financial support for faith-based groups as publicly-aided providers of domestic public services."

Following the recommendations of *Unlevel Playing Field*, White House agencies have overhauled internal procedures to help smaller religious providers to win federal discretionary grants as well as an increasing share of grants available through states and localities. This overhaul includes numerous regulatory changes, either proposed or enacted, which according to *The Expanding Administrative Presidency* "together mark a major shift in the constitutional separation of church and state." Federal job-training vouchers can now be used to earn educational credentials for religious employment. Government-forfeited properties can now be converted into houses of worship, and government funds can be used for the repair or preservation of religious buildings. Government grantees can now discriminate in hiring decisions based on religion, although this is still prohibited where statutory restrictions exist (for example, in the Workforce Investment Act of 1998) or where preempted by state or local anti-discrimination laws.

The financial stakes of the initiative are huge; its rule changes apply to $65 billion in discretionary social-service grants made by federal agencies, according to the White House. In fiscal year 2004, religious organizations received nearly 18 percent of the total dollar amount of federal discretionary social-service grants dispensed through 99 programs studied by the Roundtable on Religion and Social Welfare Policy. The total amount they received was $626 million, and 46 percent of the groups receiving these funds were new grantees. In 2005 the numbers were much higher: $2.1 billion dispensed through 130 programs, according to the White House. The Compassion Capital Fund, a capacity-building program aimed at small religious providers, distributed $148 million between 2002 and 2005.

Further rule changes are being developed to give religious providers access to the $50 billion in federal formula grants administered by states and localities. This includes, for example, $16.6 billion allocated annually to the states through Temporary Assistance for Needy Families, the government's main cash-assistance program for poor families. Today, in fact, less than 40 percent of TANF money is spent on cash assistance. Much of the money is spent on services such as child care, job training, and developing life skills. And early in 2006, Bush signed TANF-renewal legislation that earmarked $750 million over five years for promoting "healthy marriages and responsible fatherhood."

Under TANF and other programs, states have become more focused on developing partnerships with religious organizations. As of 2005, 27 states had passed legislation that included provisions to allow such partnerships; 28 had created significant administrative initiatives to encourage religious involvement in its social programs; 32 had designated an office or individual to serve as a liaison with religious groups. As a result, contract processes have been modified, contractors have been encouraged to subcontract with religious groups, and religious groups have been given capacity-building grants and technical help. Between 2002 and 2004, 16 states increased both the amount of funding and the number of grants that went to religious social-service organizations.

The White House, in turn, has undertaken major outreach efforts to activate religious involvement in the faith-based initiative. Since 2001, tens of thousands of religious leaders have attended White House–sponsored regional and national conferences designed to "take the mystery out of partnering with the federal government," as one keynote speaker put it. Many smaller training seminars and workshops have been offered through the intermediary groups financed by the Compassion Capital Fund.

Taken together, the structural and administrative changes carried out by the faith-based initiative, coupled with state-level efforts and grant-seeking mobilization on the ground, represent a massive political effort to reconstruct the social safety net around religious providers and their methods. There has been nothing like it in the history of the White House or in American social-welfare policy. Before 2001 there was no possibility of reallocating welfare resources to religious groups in any systematic way. Today there is significant progress toward that goal and significant potential for more progress. Whether future presidents will continue to expand and utilize the unique infrastructure and ethic that Bush has created is of course an open question. But the faith-based initiative has put in place important groundwork for any who would.

The significance of this transformation rests upon the fact that from the beginning the faith-based initiative has been about helping the religious groups that provide social services, not the people who depend on them. Thus, it was never a social policy of any kind: poor people and poor communities are merely its imputed beneficiaries. It is no coincidence that the only new funding stream created by the faith-based initiative when it was launched, the Compassion Capital Fund, was established to "increase the scale and effectiveness" of religious groups and to give them more government funding. This has always been the primary measuring stick of success in President Bush's new version of the war on poverty.

But before we can fully understand the faith-based initiative and judge its success for ourselves, we must look back to its intellectual origins.

5

THE CONCEPT OF SPHERE SOVEREIGNTY first emerged in the Netherlands in a mid-19th-century struggle over the public funding of religious schools. The struggle began with a campaign led by orthodox Calvinists against a Liberal education bill; in 1879 Abraham Kuyper, who dubbed the bill *decretum horribile*, founded the Anti-Revolutionary Party in support of the cause. The ARP was the Netherlands' first mass political party and would become an important national vehicle for Kuyper's ideas about religious autonomy within the liberal state.

Kuyper's June 8, 1877, editorial in *De Standaard* provides a lucid summary of the party's tenets:

1. The idea that people decide what is normative in life (called popular sovereignty) is opposed to the Word of God, which teaches that God is sovereign as the final lawgiver.

2. Christians confess the relevance of God's Word even for politics, rejecting a vague concept of natural law or human reason.

3. The office of the state has been ordained to be God's minister for justice through the conscience of public officials who believe in his ordinances.

4. Educational responsibility rests with parents and not with the state. The idea that, for financial reasons, Christian people have only a secularist public school open to them must be rejected.

5. A Christian political movement such as the Anti-Revolutionary Party must maintain its independence (from all forms of humanism and nonbiblical political views), based on the Bible.

Reformed and Catholic groups worked together to solicit 460,000 signatures in opposition to the education bill—nearly four times the size of the entire Dutch electorate at the time—but the bill passed nonetheless. Still, after this, the ARP collaborated more and more with its Catholic counterparts, working to expand the then-limited franchise. This *Unio Mystica*, as Kuyper termed it, was seen as a "monstrous alliance" by the Liberals. In 1888 it won its first majority in the lower house of parliament.

At the same time that Kuyper was forming the ARP, he was also founding the Free

University of Amsterdam, at whose opening in 1880 he gave a speech putting sphere sovereignty at the center of confessional politics. In 1901 Anti-Revolutionaries installed Kuyper as prime minister, a position he held until 1905. After further struggle and a series of incremental gains, the coalition won a decisive constitutional victory for the public funding of religious schools in 1917.

Kuyper was both anti-socialist and anti-individualist. He believed that social order and human flourishing within and through this order are rooted in divinely ordained structures that compose a "natural" community that is theologically and morally prior to the state (whether it is democratic or not). The family, the church, charitable associations, and confessional schools—intermediary structures between the individual and the state—are elements of this natural community and are as fully real as individual persons. Government institutions, programs, and rules form the political community, through which the larger natural order is coordinated and kept in balance.

In more conventional, pietistic theology, the political realm arises with the fall into sin and is viewed negatively, as a deterrent to violence and destruction in the postlapsarian world. Kuyper embraced a more positive view of the state. In his Free University speech he said, citing Proverbs 29:4, that the state "gives stability to the land by justice" but that "public justice" is a coordinating, subsidiary power. Apart from shared needs such as national defense and infrastructure, the state should uphold "sovereignty in one's own circle" (*souvereiniteit in eigen kring*).

Kuyper's present-day followers regard him as part of a broader "pluralist" movement in political thought that flourished in the early decades of the 20th century as an alternative to individualist and statist traditions. The central principle of this movement was that self-regulating associations were essential to the health of communities and democracy, both as sources of social cohesion for individuals and as a "bulwark of liberty" against encroachments of the central state.

The most sophisticated exponents of this view were the English pluralists John Neville Figgis, Harold Laski, and G.D.H. Cole. The last two, already skeptical of the state, extended their skepticism to employers and the market. In the 1920s they defended guild-socialist ideas such as workplace democracy and community economic control against statist currents within the Labour Party, until the worldwide depression of the

1930s brought practical hopes for economic democracy to an end.

The faith-based initiative is pluralist in its emphasis on the public importance of self-governing religious associations. But unlike earlier pluralist movements, it ignores the free market's homogenizing, destructive control in many communities and the inordinate power of employers.

Kuyper himself believed in a limited state, but he did not ignore the market. His limited state is not the night-watchman state of classical liberalism, whose role is to protect property, enforce contracts, ensure competitive markets, and provide basic public goods. Instead, the state exists to protect and enable the natural community in its ordered "spheres of influence." Political community falters when it violates sphere sovereignty, thus intruding on a society in which God has already spoken. When it fails to respect the separate associational spheres, the state violates its limited but essential purpose of maintaining public justice—proper order between the autonomous spheres of the natural community.

It was on this foundation that "pillarization" (*verzuiling*) was established in the Netherlands in the early 20th century. Each individual pillar—Catholic, Calvinist, or socialist—is made of interlocking organizations that provide services from childhood to old age—each according to its unique cultural perspective. The pillars, the sociologist Göran Therborn writes, are "bent on defending a separate social world against the state, not least against the liberal state." Successful pillarization "presupposes a weak central state and involves a political perspective of a marginal or subsidiary state."

Pillarization and sphere sovereignty both derive from a broader "federalist" legacy rooted in the historical experience of minority religious communities in Catholic and Lutheran states. The foundation was laid by the German legal philosopher Johannes Althusius (1557–1638). The magistrate of Emden, one of the first German cities to embrace the Reformed faith, Althusius developed a theory of "consociational" federalism, in which the state is essentially a compact among self-governing but interdependent communities. Althusius was also an exponent of Protestant "resistance theory," a doctrine of popular sovereignty that influenced the Huguenots, the Scottish Covenanters, and the English Puritans (it played a significant role in the execution of Charles I in 1649). But subsidiarity proved more enduring than resistance theory, as direct oppression by state churches was replaced by the marginalizing influence of the secular modern state. For many churches, a theory of the subsidiary state—placing limits on state functions and assigning a positive role to religious communities—was necessary to secure their place amid the expanding competencies of modern welfare and education systems.

Kuyper's concept of sphere sovereignty maintains the Althusian idea of common purpose among self-governing units. Families, churches, and other structures that intermediate between individuals and the state must submit to justice—as enforced by the state—in respecting each other's boundaries and fulfilling obligations to their members (fulfilling, that is, their public purposes). But each is nevertheless, as Kuyper wrote, "ruled by another authority that descends directly from God." Kuyper held that the secularism and individualism of the French Revolution threatened to destroy the natural community by elevating individuals and allying them, through individual rights, with the secular state—thus the response of the Anti-Revolutionary Party in defense of confessional schools. Public education was part of the disintegrative revolutionary spirit, epitomized in France by the Chapelier ordinance of 1791 banning trade guilds, the anticlerical doctrine of *laïcisme*, and the state annexation of Catholic schools.

No earthly authority, Kuyper wrote in *De Standaard*, "can ever assert itself contrary to the obedience we owe God ... or nullify the authority with which others are clothed in their own spheres." Family and religion, arts and trades—each has its own proper role and sovereign order as instilled by the laws of creation. The role of the state is to provide the "justice"—the ordering power—that protects the distinct social spheres but has no authority within them.

Kuyperians today insist that sphere sovereignty requires not mere separateness but "principled pluralism," a world of self-governing religious differences protected and supported by the state. There can be no favoritism of one faith over another or of all faiths over no faith: Kuyper opposed a state religion or religious requirements for citizenship. In a world of cultural self-governance, liberals see a faltering common purpose and even factional dangers. Kuyperians, on the other hand, see a kind of organic order without hierarchy, where the autonomy of the parts ensures the order of the whole.

For the architects of the faith-based initiative, sphere sovereignty supports an attractive ideal of religious self-governance in social welfare. But history reveals another side to this ideal. Kuyper's thought influenced Afrikaner racial nationalism and, more particularly, the Dutch Reformed Church's theology of racial separation under apartheid. Recent scholarship has shown how Afrikaner theology selectively appropriated and distorted Kuyper's themes, and a movement of black Reformed Christians in South Africa has worked since the early 1980s to reclaim the liberative aspects of Dutch Calvinism and the Kuyperian tradition. But serious questions remain about the possible dangers of sphere sovereignty and other similar doctrines in pitting social groups against one another or in justifying social hierarchies.

Critics of this type of strong "value pluralism," as the political scientist William Galston has termed it, point to the dark side of group values as exemplified by racial-supremacy movements, sectarian violence, and anti-immigration activism. In Europe, many anti-immigration movements, some with roots in fascism, have more or less abandoned racial ideology in favor of cultural differentiation and even multiculturalism. These are extreme examples, but they reflect the problems of a strong value pluralism that undermines universalistic concepts such as human rights; the political scientist Stephen Macedo argues that such a system may also weaken the "democratic authority to make public policy." The Bush administration's efforts to reassure the public that minority religions will not be excluded from the faith-based initiative reveals one area where these dangers clearly still exist.

6

THE REMARKABLE STORY OF HOW A religious theory of the limited state came to influence American social policy begins with the Center for Public Justice. Founded in the mid-1970s, the Center aspires to "Serve God, Advance Justice, and Transform Public Life." With deep confessional roots in the Reformed tradition stretching back to John Calvin, the Center is especially influenced by Dutch Calvinism and by Abraham Kuyper in particular. James Skillen, the long-time executive director of the Center and now its president, studied philosophy at the Free University of Amsterdam, which Kuyper founded. The Center began as the Association for Public Justice, a membership organization that sought to build a Christian political movement. Today it focuses on "foundational" research mainly in the area of social welfare. It seeks to produce a "public philosophy of human responsibility that is at once both individual and corporate," working from a "justice viewpoint grounded in biblical assumptions about human nature and responsibility."

The Center's involvement in the faith-based initiative grew out of an earlier project, conducted in the mid-1990s, "Welfare Responsibility: An Inquiry into the Roots of America's Welfare Policy Crisis." This was the most significant attempt to date to develop a consistent Christian model of welfare reform. In 1996, when Bush was still governor of Texas, one of his top aides, Don Willett, attended a Center for Public Justice conference on charitable choice. There he met Stanley Carlson-Thies, then the director of the Center's welfare-responsibility project. Carlson-Thies became a regular adviser to Willett and Bush, who were trying to implement charitable choice in Texas. When Bush was elected president, Carlson-Thies helped them develop a federal version of the policy and worked closely with the Bush-Cheney transition team to establish the White House Office of Faith-Based and Community Initiatives. Early in 2001 he was appointed associate director of law and policy of the White House office, where he was chiefly responsible for supervising the departmental charitable-choice audits President Bush ordered shortly after being inaugurated. A serious thinker with moderate political leanings, Carlson-Thies returned to the Center after leaving the White House in the spring of 2002.

(A Ph.D. in political science, Carlson-Thies wrote his 500-page dissertation on the theory and development of government support for confessional subcultures in the Netherlands.)

A detailed 2004 study, *Of Little Faith: The Politics of George W. Bush's Faith-Based Initiatives*, singles out the Center as "deeply involved" in a movement of "sympathetic constitutional scholars and lawyers" who, in the wake of the conservative takeover of Congress in 1994, "helped the politicians fashion legal arguments to support greater cooperation between the government and religious providers of social services." This understates the Center's formative role. Carlson-Thies and Skillen helped Carl Esbeck develop charitable choice, and Esbeck has worked closely with the Center on numerous publications and projects. Esbeck was appointed director of the task force on faith-based initiatives in the Department of Justice in 2001 and was the constitutional point man for the faith-based initiative during Bush's first term. Another important advocate is the Center's former associate director Luis Lugo. He is now the director of the Pew Forum on Religion and Public Life, the major Washington institution for journalists covering the faith-based initiative and other church–state issues. Lugo also edited a significant volume of essays, *Religion, Pluralism, and Public Life*, assessing Kuyper's legacy for the 21st century.

Other affiliates who have done influential work related to the faith-based initiative include Amy Sherman, a well-known advocate for religious social services, now with the Sagamore Institute; Stephen Monsma, a Pepperdine political scientist and a leading expert on government contracting with religious groups; and Charles Glenn, a Boston University education professor and the author of *The Ambiguous Embrace: Government and Faith-Based Schools and Social Agencies*—a little-noticed but important study that is the first to detail the Christian Democratic model behind charitable choice and the faith-based initiative.

Interestingly, Kuyper's influence is growing within the wider religious right. The attorney Jay Sekulow, whose American Center for Law and Justice is the leading legal organization of the religious right, cites Kuyper as "one of my favorite theologians." Sekulow follows a cultural-mandate approach, as set out in Kuyper's best-known proclamation of world-view theology: "There is not one square inch in the whole domain of our human existence over which Christ, who is Sovereign, does not cry out, 'Mine!'" Charles Colson, a close friend and ally of President Bush, is an avowed world-view Christian in the Kuyperian mold. As Colson wrote in a 2000 article, "Christians must recognize this in order to know the fullness of life in Christ, to be able to formulate a defense of Christian truth in every single area of life, and to begin taking back our culture in the name of the King of kings." It was Colson who gave Michael Gerson his start in public affairs right out of Wheaton College, the "evangelical Harvard"; Gerson became a speechwriter for Senator Dan Coats and later for Bush.

The rise of Abraham Kuyper to his prominent role in welfare reform really began in the early 1980s, long before charitable choice or anything comparable had emerged from the religious right. This was the age of the Human Life Amendment, the Moral Majority, and Pat Robertson's presidential bid. Yet as early as 1981, Reformed scholars in evangelical legal circles began to formulate the concepts now enshrined in the faith-based initiative.

It was in that year that Bernard Zylstra, a Dutch Calvinist philosopher and the first president of the Institute for Christian Studies in Toronto (he also served on Carlson-Thies's doctoral committee), published an essay that made a prescient case for government funding of religious social services. Based on a speech first delivered before the Christian Legal Society, the essay drew on the concept of "mediating structures" popularized by Peter Berger and Richard John

Neuhaus's 1977 book *To Empower People.* Zylstra posed the problem of religious welfare provision in essentially the same terms that would be ratified 15 years later by charitable choice. He wrote that the concerns of religious "caring institutions" overlap with those of the state and asked, "Does this overlap mean that the religious character of these mediating structures must be eradicated as soon as the state becomes involved, especially when public funds are used?"

His answer is striking: "The solution I am advocating," he wrote, "is *the disestablishment of secularism* in the mediating structures on the part of every level of government and *the equal protection of the free exercise of religion* in these structures." Going beyond the Supreme Court's now-reigning neutrality logic in direct-aid cases, Zylstra argued that religious providers' free exercise of religion must be fully protected in federal contracting regimes. (As noted earlier, Carl Esbeck argues that the logic of neutrality theory, as it stands today, naturally leads to permitting government funding of pervasively religious social services.)

Strikingly, the welfare-reform consensus that began to crystallize in the late 1980s and culminated in 1996 did not propose or even address government funding of religious social-service providers. The influential 1987 "new consensus" report of the Working Seminar on Family and American Welfare Policy, led by Michael Novak, instead recommended that "religious social agencies should help to focus the resources of society upon the moral dimensions of dependency." Only a few years before charitable choice became law, most leading conservatives still apparently believed that religion should play a private role, not a public role, in social welfare.

More extreme religious conservatives, however, inspired by Charles Murray's 1984 anti-government tract *Losing Ground,* were drawing on Kuyperian themes to advance an explicitly theocratic version of welfare reform. In the late 1980s George Grant, a mentor to Marvin Olasky, published a series of books on "biblical welfare." Focusing on "the communal actors and activities that the Biblical commands place at the center of our loyalties: family and church," Grant envisioned an army of churches arising from the ashes of welfare reform and establishing a beachhead for wider Christian dominion. He believed that public programs should be dismantled and religious charity renewed: "Government cannot get *out* of the way if the church does not get *in* the way."

In fact, like many of Bush's religious advisers a decade later, particularly Olasky, Grant proposed charity tax credits as the most effective tool of welfare reform, even proposing the establishment of church-appointed certification boards to insure the legitimacy of participating institutions—an innovation Bush himself later adopted in Texas. Unlike Bush, however, Grant openly conceived of charity tax credits as an endgame strategy of "public-to-private transfer."

In 1992 a group of mainly Presbyterian intellectuals and church leaders, including Grant, gathered at the Covenant Presbyterian Church in Oak Ridge, Tennessee, to develop a vision of welfare reform based on biblical principles. In a 1994 volume of essays drawn from the conference, David Hall, the church's senior pastor, proposed a sequence of devolutionary steps for replacing public welfare with religious charity. Among other things, he proposed that welfare spending be administered experimentally by the states through a block-grant system (this would come to pass in the welfare-reform bill of 1996). He also called for a transitional phase of government subsidies for religious providers before "finally weaning expectations for welfare away from statist agencies." "Let the Church be the Church" is the "rallying cry for welfare reform," Hall added, quoting George Grant. "Perhaps the regulators can overlook the imagined 'wall of separation' ... liberating the church to once again do her job."

The Christian Democratic influences that would later dominate—especially the Dutch Calvinist variant represented by the Center for Public Justice—and the Reformed "dominionism" of Grant, Olasky, Colson, and others on the far right have common theological roots. The Center for Public Justice, however, advances a distinctly pluralistic version of world-view theology, which it argues is consistent with Kuyper's own views. Kuyper did in fact advance a pluralistic vision of religious self-governance, but to some degree this arose from the unique political circumstances of the Netherlands in the late 19th century. At that time, different churches were putting aside their historical antagonisms to work together against the common foe of secular liberalism.

7

THE CATHOLIC CONCEPT OF SUBSID-
iarity, like sphere sovereignty, offered a
vision of a social order that could stand
against secularization. It, too, influenced
the development of the faith-based initiative. Conservative Catholics, like their
Reformed counterparts, saw the emerging
consensus on welfare reform in the 1990s
as an opportunity to apply their beliefs to
public life.

In 1984 the Lay Commission on Catholic Social Teaching and the U.S. Economy
published *Toward the Future*, a preemptive

attack on the U.S. Catholic Bishops' "welfarist" pastoral letter, *Economic Justice for All*, which was then being drafted. Michael Joyce, a member of the commission who would go on to play a leading role in conservative philanthropy as the head of the Lynde and Harry Bradley Foundation, lectured audiences at Yale and other institutions about the bishops' "bad economics."

In a recollection of that effort published in *Crisis* magazine in 1996, Joyce suggests that *Economic Justice for All*, which recommended that states intervene when markets fail, had applied the doctrine of subsidiarity incorrectly. Rather than requiring public programs to improve social conditions, subsidiarity, according to Joyce, requires a dismantling of public programs. Government must retreat because "no national or international economic policy or power of government has even a fraction of the capacity to dignify the human person that is possessed by the den mothers and Little League coaches of our communities." As the head of the Bradley Foundation from 1985 to 2001, Joyce would do more than anyone else in conservative philanthropy to promote faith-based initiatives, which he described in a 2001 lecture as a "new science of public administration."

Bush publicly unveiled the faith-based initiative in July 1999 during his first major campaign speech, "The Duty of Hope." This speech, written with the help of John DiIulio, Marvin Olasky, and other religious advisers, sparked the interest of Catholic commentators, who widely noted the relevance of Catholic doctrine to the proposed initiative. Subsidiarity emerged as a term of art for religious approaches to welfare reform and social policy. George F. Will, for example, put subsidiarity front and center in a column published shortly after Bush launched the faith-based initiative in January 2001. Jesse Helms called for a religious foreign-aid system based on subsidiarity, an idea Bush may have had in mind when he established an office of the faith-based initiative in the U.S. Agency for International Development in December 2002. Influential Catholic advisers to the Bush administration, such as Deal Hudson of *Crisis* magazine and Paul Weyrich of the Free Congress Foundation, were vocal proponents of the faith-based initiative, arguing that government must adhere to the doctrine of subsidiarity to be effective. John DiIulio, a self-proclaimed born-again Catholic, characterized "The Duty of Hope" as a "blueprint for applied subsidiarity."

Subsidiarity is best known today in the secular, federalist version enshrined in the Maastricht Treaty of the European Union, which says that "the Community shall take action, in accordance with the principle of subsidiarity, only if and in so far as the objectives of the proposed action cannot be sufficiently achieved by the Member States and can therefore, by reason of the scale or effects of the proposed action, be better achieved by the Community." Like sphere sovereignty, however, this concept of social order was originally theological. James Skillen argues that subsidiarity resembles sphere sovereignty but embraces a more hierarchical concept of social order and the role of the state. It is a "corporate" doctrine of part and whole, with the parts being harmonized in a higher unity, an idea reaching back within Catholic thought to Thomas Aquinas.

The central document in this tradition is Pius XI's 1931 encyclical *Quadragesimo Anno*. The "40th year" of the title refers back to Leo XIII's 1891 encyclical *Rerum Novarum*, which promoted workplace reforms, capital-labor reconciliation, and Catholic worker organizations and thus played an important role in salvaging the Church from anti-modernist currents that favored socialism in the competition for working-class loyalty. The document's notable silence on democracy—despite its modernizing sensibility—foreshadows the Church's alliances with fascism in the 1920s and 1930s at the expense of the "common enemies" of liberalism and socialism, which were routinely attacked in official teaching.

Even before *Rerum Novarum* thrust the Church into modern class politics, however, Leo XIII formulated a theory that would greatly influence the development of European welfare systems in the 20th century, especially the German system. *Immortale Dei*, issued in 1885, defined the basic problem in a way that was strikingly similar to Kuyper's earlier articulation of sphere sovereignty. But *Immortale Dei* paid very particular attention to the problems arising when church and state both have legitimate jurisdiction in a given social domain—education and welfare being the most important examples:

> Inasmuch as each of these two powers has authority over the same subjects, and as it might come to pass that one and the same thing … might belong to the jurisdiction and determination of both, therefore God …who is the author of these two powers, has marked out the course of each in right correlation to the other. "For the powers that are, are ordained of God."

To preserve the church's legitimate claims in social areas increasingly addressed by the state, the "right correlation," according to the Leonine model, was subsidiarity. Community institutions—particularly the family and the church—are the more proximate, and therefore the more natural, institutions of social support. Thus, the state must delegate core social tasks to these institutions and give them autonomy.

Subsidiarity's controlling passage, from *Quadragesimo Anno*, has a strong devolutionary thrust that many commentators today relate to welfare reform and the faith-based initiative:

> Just as it is gravely wrong to take from individuals what they can accomplish by their own initiative and industry and give it to the community, so also it is an injustice and at

the same time a grave evil and disturbance of right order to assign to a greater and higher association what lesser and subordinate organizations can do. For every social activity ought of its very nature to furnish help to the members of the body social, and never destroy and absorb them.

Yet commentators generally ignore the corporatist, hierarchical vision that emerges in the passage that follows:

Therefore, those in power should be sure that the more perfectly a graduated order is kept among the various associations, in observance of the principle of the "subsidiary function," the stronger social authority and effectiveness will be, and the happier and more prosperous the condition of the state.

As James Skillen has said, subsidiarity puts the family and the church back in charge of the things that fall within their natural domains, but the ultimate good in this vision of graduated powers is the unified corporate order of medieval theology.

Authoritarian governments openly drew on subsidiarity and Catholic corporatism in the 1930s. The short-lived one-party clerical regime of Engelbert Dollfuss in Austria, for example, modeled its constitution directly on the teachings of *Quadragesimo Anno* and was embraced by the Vatican through a diplomatic concordat. The Portuguese dictator António de Oliveira Salazar based his 40-year Estado Novo on a similar interpretation of Catholic principles.

A more recent connection is with Gianfranco Fini's Alleanza Nazionale in Italy, the second power in Silvio Berlusconi's ruling coalition from 2001 to 2006. With explicit historical roots in Italian fascism, Fini's party, formerly called the Movimento Sociale Italiano, was reborn in electoral politics in the mid-1990s and established a new program that modulated key elements of its fascist legacy. The political scientist Mario Sznajder argues that this makeover was designed to position the Alleanza Nazionale as a more traditional right-wing party in the mold of the Gaullist and British Conservative parties and, to some extent, the American New Right. Like the faith-based initiative, its program invoked subsidiarity as a policy principle needed to secure the restoration of civil society. As Sznajder notes, "Civil society, according to this ideology, would play a central role by taking over from the state all the functions various voluntary associations—social, economic, cultural—

could perform with greater efficiency than state bureaucracies ... These ideas revolve around the central role of the family as the basic social unit, within the framework of Catholic morality."

Some features of the faith-based initiative suggest a corporatist sensibility closer to Germany's approach. The Compassion Capital Fund delegates federal grant-making powers to a group of large intermediary structures. Such structures, one White House official suggested, could be the "engine of the faith-based initiative." This is where changes in governance make a large difference: it is one thing for religious social-service providers to be intermediaries between the government and individuals, as subsidiarity prescribes; it is something else entirely for coordinating intermediaries to arise between religious providers and the government. The latter is a hallmark of corporatism and would add significant scale and influence to the religious self-governance restored by charitable choice.

Some have suggested that a series of large intermediary institutions could help frontline providers, not only in coordinating services and identifying needs but in working with government in pursuit of their own shared institutional needs—not least of all, certainly, a steady flow of funds. Although still in embryonic form, this idea is suggestive of the "peak associations" common to corporatist polities. The Compassion Capital Fund directed about $95 million to 44 such intermediaries from 2002 to 2004.

In an extraordinary commentary issued on March 13, 2001, shortly after Bush took office, Paul Weyrich, the chairman of the conservative Free Congress Foundation, describes a phone call with Karl Rove, Bush's top political advisor, in which he told Rove that Bush has "mastered the art of Catholic governance." Rove added that Bush "understands the Catholic principle of subsidiarity." The approbation is precise, based not on a laundry-list of issues, but on a shared concept of the state. Again, this emphasis on governance is something unique even in the vaunted political history of the religious right. The transfer of resources to religious groups is no simple privatization scheme if it also transfers public authority to religion.

8

EMBOLDENED BY THE WELFARE-REFORM consensus forged during the Clinton years, the faith-based initiative has succeeded in transforming the very foundations of the debate on poverty. The secular welfare state was once regarded as the main (if weak and fragmented) bulwark against America's unbridled inequality and barbaric levels of impoverishment and imprisonment. Today we are told that the main problem for poor communities is the secularism of social services. If the war on poverty was really a "war on God," as Marvin Olasky has said, then establishing a new class of religious social-service providers may be the only way to save the poor. The consensus has found its philosophy.

But more than philosophy will be needed. In 2003, the United States had a higher GDP, with 100 million fewer people, than the 15 core countries of the European Union combined. Yet as a percentage of GDP, the United States spends less on social transfers (welfare, unemployment, pensions, health care, and housing) than Portugal, the poorest country of the group. The faith-based initiative does nothing to close this gaping hole. As of 2003, nearly 49 million people lived near or below the federal poverty line in the United States, and the numbers have risen since then.

A startling fact puts all this in perspective. When you compare the United States to those European countries where the principles of Bush's faith-based initiative have actually governed, you find that these also happen to be among the least impoverished and most equal countries in the world. Germany and the Netherlands are good examples, as the political scientist Kees van Kersbergen documents in his 1995 book *Social Capitalism: A Study of Christian Democracy and the Welfare State*. As he notes in his introduction, Christian Democracy is poorly understood and little studied, even within Europe. Yet it ruled significant portions of Europe for substantial periods after World War II, with particular strength in Germany, the Netherlands, Belgium, and Italy. The German and Dutch systems in particular—very different from Nordic social democracies— were carefully constructed on the principles of subsidiarity and sphere sovereignty. Much of the thinking behind these welfare systems was inherited from earlier religious struggles against liberalism and fascism.

In 1917, sphere sovereignty was enshrined in the Dutch constitution in the form of public support for religious schools. The famous Article 23 says that "all persons shall be free to provide education"—to found schools and direct education based on varying philosophies. Secondly, "Private primary schools ... shall be financed from public funds according to the same standards as public-authority schools." Today approximately 69 percent of Dutch primary students and 73 percent of secondary students attend private schools financed by the government; an estimated one third of all primary-school students attend religious schools. As noted earlier, public support for religious education was replicated in other areas to form the Dutch system of pillar-ization—predominant in health care, social services, and even broadcasting through the 1960s. In short, the Dutch welfare system was embedded in a coherent social order, one that put the market, no less than the state, in its proper place. No comparable structures or ideas of social order took root in the United States.

Although many Dutch social agencies still maintain a religious identity, pillariza-tion began to unravel in the 1970s, owing in part to the strong countercultural cur-rents that were sweeping through Europe. Today being served from cradle to grave by a single confessional pillar is rare; people tend to shop around based on factors other than religion, such as quality and location. De-pillarization was confirmed by the merger, in the late 1970s, of the ARP and the Catholic

People's Party to form the Christian Democratic Appeal. But confessional alignments remain an important force. As Stephen Monsma notes, the Christian Democratic Appeal or its forbears were part of every government from 1918 to 1994.

Dutch Catholics supported the growth of a comprehensive welfare state after World War II, often in alignment with the Dutch Labor Party. The ARP, however, struggled internally over the rise of the Dutch *verzorgingsstaat*, or "caring state," with some leaders and many members fearing a depletion of Calvinist identity. In the 1960s, progressive ARP leaders, claiming the mantle of the young Kuyper, adopted a more prophetic stance of "social solidarity" with the oppressed, pushing for increased welfare spending and more aid for international development.

One interesting point raised by critics of the faith-based initiative is that countries that finance religious institutions—the example of England is often cited—are typically much more secular than the United States. The Netherlands' secularization is particularly illuminating here, given the confessional churches' defeat of liberalism in the early 20th century and the subsequent pillarization of Dutch politics and society. In 1995, only 55 percent of people in the Netherlands said that they believed in God, compared to over 90 percent in the United States. A poll by the Barna Group showed that 43 percent of Americans in 2004 attended church the previous week, although some scholars believe that regular church attendance is probably closer to 30 percent. The comparable figure for the Netherlands is about 16 percent.

Advocates of the faith-based initiative influenced by the Dutch theory and model are particularly aware of these trends and have sought to address them. Charles Glenn, for example, devotes substantial attention to this question in *The Ambiguous Embrace*, putting the onus for desecularizing the social safety net on religious providers rather than government. Government interference is only part of the problem, he says. Religious providers "are also faced with the more subtle danger of self-betrayal, voluntary abandonment of their original purpose." In fact, this is an "even greater threat" than government—an increasingly plausible argument today. Glenn quotes an unnamed member of John Ashcroft's Senate staff who, in the early days of charitable choice, told a group of leaders of faith-based organizations that "there is nothing from a governmental level that we can do to prevent you from corrupting yourself." One of the most significant political dynamics of the faith-based initiative is revealed here: the task of getting religious groups to actually serve the religious goals of the initiative. Glenn thus outlines not only how government should behave "to avoid spoiling their distinctive character and contribution" but also how religious groups should "protect themselves from interference with their core mission and distinctive character."

The religious leaders who have banked on subsidiarity and sphere sovereignty rather than more direct privatization clearly face a daunting task. But some groups are seizing the opportunity to reconnect their religious mission with their social services. For example, the plaintiffs in *Lown v. Salvation Army*, employees of the Army's Social Services for Children agency in the New York City area, alleged discriminatory conduct growing out of something called the One Army Concept. Launched in 2003, this effort aims to create a more homogeneous, evangelical work force and message in the Army's social ministries.

9

LIKE THE NETHERLANDS, GERMANY has a strong legal tradition of protecting the religious autonomy of government contractors, and it also has a well-funded, comprehensive welfare system. This system, which has absorbed, on average, 25 percent of GDP since 1980, is essentially the historical product of Christian Democratic rule combined with pressures from the social-democratic left. The extensive role of religious social-service providers in Germany is largely a story of Catholic subsidiarity, and the result is a neo-corporatist system dominated by six large umbrella organizations: the *freie Wohlfahrtsverbände*, or free welfare associations. The two largest of these are religious—Catholic and Protestant.

The German welfare system emerged from a struggle that began in the 1920s, when the Weimar Republic embraced an approach to poverty known as *soziale Fürsorge*, or social relief. Unlike charity, social relief emphasized external conditions, preventive measures, and, increasingly, social insurance against market forces. Throughout the 1920s Catholic and Protestant charities fought bitterly against both liberal and fascist constructions of centralized welfare in what one scholar calls a *Kulturkampf* ("culture war"). At the core of this *Kulturkampf* there was a *Weltanschauungskampf*, or battle of world views. As one confessional leader wrote in 1931,

Social work has become the great, decisive area of a cultural conflict, a violent struggle for hegemony and dominance between the Christian confessions and the irreligious, anti-ecclesiastical worldviews ... The time when everyone believed that welfare could confidently be left to the state is at an end.

A 1923 law introduced regulations recognizing seven *Spitzenverbände* (umbrella organizations) as "peak associations"—essentially, intermediaries between the public welfare system and the private religious providers. But individual states and municipalities allowed varying degrees of religious involvement and autonomy, which led the peak associations to form a national league that could speak with one voice and establish uniform subsidiary governance throughout all levels of the welfare system.

Religious exclusion from public welfare became an essential feature of the Nazi critique of Weimar liberalism, and the Nazi seizure of power was generally welcomed by the confessional antagonists of liberal welfare. In a haunting prefiguration of our own welfare-reform disputes today, some confessional leaders saw the collapse of Weimar liberalism as vindication of a religious world view that emphasized duties and self-reliance over rights and economic justice. In 1933, the Nazis declared Christianity the "unshakeable foundation of the ethical and moral life of our people," denouncing the expansion of public welfare during the Weimar Republic as an attempt to exclude the churches and dispense with Christian charity. But the Nazis did not restore religion to public life; while churches retained some autonomy in education, they were rapidly pushed out of welfare as the Nazis redefined it along eugenic lines.

After World War II, something very close to the corporatist welfare system envisioned by confessional leaders of the 1920s was finally realized in Germany. Now revived in a form that excluded authoritarianism, subsidiarity was enshrined in at least two separate laws: the Social Assistance Act of 1961 and the Social Code of 1976. These laws required "public bodies responsible for social assistance" to enlist churches, religious communities, and the free welfare associations while acknowledging "their independence in the targeting and execution of their functions."

Charitable choice is essentially the same thing; in fact, as the social scientists Lester Salamon and Helmut Anheier argue, the German and American systems are superficially quite similar. Both rely extensively on non-governmental providers. Responsibilities are divided between the public and nonprofit sectors: the public responsibility is to authorize and finance social programs, whereas private responsibility governs the delivery of services or benefits.

But Germany's subsidiary welfare state is different from that of the United States in almost every other respect. The American system is fragmented and pragmatic, a "polyarchic" patchwork of compromises and interests. The German social laws, in contrast, require government consultation with the free welfare associations. The result is a centralized consultative apparatus for policy development, bearing little resemblance to Washington's partisan advocacy. This could change if the Compassion Capital Fund further employs new institutional "intermediaries," but any significant shift in power away from the Republican Party is likely to undermine that goal.

Germany and the Netherlands are key examples of what van Kersbergen calls the Christian Democratic model of social capitalism. This approach, he writes, stresses the "autonomy of social organizations in a plural society" yet is founded "on some notion of harmony" between groups or classes in society. The original impetus for Christian Democracy was to forestall class struggle by promoting cooperation between capital and labor. But the cornerstone ideal is the prospering family, with its natural capacities and obligations. Public services are troubling, then, because they substitute abstract dependency for family duty. The proper role of a caring state is to modify the wage system to guarantee a living family wage. Family allowances, a minimum social income, and unemployment and pension benefits with high replacement rates are hallmarks of this system. The role of the state is to help families when they cannot help themselves rather than displace their natural functions when they can, or blame them when things go badly.

The fundamental mechanism of Christian Democracy is the social transfer of income; van Kersbergen writes that its goal is to "moderate the outcome of the logic of the imperfect market by transferring considerable sums of money to families and other social institutions in need." A policy of full employment is not ideal because it reaches too far in adjusting social structures. Where markets fail, social transfers rehabilitate families and communities to the material level appropriate to their needs and dignity. Where social services are necessary for emergencies or temporary needs, the subsidiary function, approximating as much as possible a family approach, is the standard. "Privately governed, publicly financed welfare arrangements are the ideal," van Kersbergen writes.

Sphere sovereignty and subsidiarity require independent social-service providers and neutral funding of even the most religious. But these principles do not operate in a social vacuum, and the primary goal is not to help churches get a larger share of welfare resources, as with the faith-based initiative. On the contrary, what makes subsidiarity in social services something other than charity is the comprehensive system of social transfers that backs it up, guaranteeing a living family wage in good times and bad. A subsidiary welfare state is not necessarily weak or inactive; it is limited only in the sense that it does not usurp or constrain the traditional role of religion in society. Christian Democracy repudiates charity in favor of the public transfer of resources; comparative results with the United States are striking.

On average, American social spending is about 40 percent lower than in either Christian or social democracies, and the poverty rate is nearly twice as high. In the ten-year period following 1984, the United States had less "pre-government" or "market" poverty than Germany and only slightly more that the Netherlands. Yet "post-government" poverty in the United States—poverty after transfers and taxes—was much higher. Over ten years, the percentage reduction in overall poverty in the United States from pre-government to post-government was only around 20 percent, while in Germany it was nearly 70 percent and in the Netherlands it was over 90 percent.

The reason for these countries' success is obvious: both devote significantly more of their national budgets to social spending, or, as one recent study put it, "social transfers matter." Whether public commitments strengthen or weaken traditional community is a question of benefit types and the structure of services—who provides them—not their finances. Without adequate finances, on the other hand, justice is fundamentally denied.

Critics of secularism who care about poverty should take note of an important contradiction. Catholic and Kuyperian social thought were anti-modern in their attitudes toward the secular state, but they were also anti-capitalist in supporting organized challenges to employer domination, such as trade unions, as well as substantial public assistance to ensure human welfare and dignity where markets fail. Growing poverty was unmistakable evidence of moral decline and political degeneracy, a time when small numbers of wealthy men were able, as Leo XIII observed, "to lay upon the teeming masses of the laboring poor a yoke little better than that of slavery itself."

Kuyper might point out that the difference between reducing poverty by 20 percent and by 90 percent is theologically paramount, and that it is morally irrelevant if the church regains autonomy over its social services while poverty grows. He saw poverty as a type of oppression and abuse by a market system, and as a dangerous enemy of faith. Those who claim to be addressing poverty "do not honor God's word," he declared, if they "ever forget how the Christ (just as his prophets before him and his apostles after him) invariably took sides against those who were powerful and living in luxury, and for the suffering and oppressed."

One looks in vain for even the faintest practical echo of these prophetic ideas in Bush's faith-based initiative. The social-spending cuts and caps of the 2006 federal budget, and the further cuts proposed for 2007, reinforce the cynical view that Bush is using religion as a cover for withdrawing government aid to the poor. But this underestimates poverty's *political* role, as a platform for religion and for a Republican Party that is trying to consolidate power by further eroding the Democratic base. A social safety net financed by the public but governed by religion has obvious political advantages over leaving everything to private charity.

More on the order of a regime change than a withdrawal of support, it remains to be seen if this is simply a transitional policy on the way to terminating government aid to poor communities, as some suspect. What is certain is that any such withdrawal would betray the religious concepts of the state that animate the faith-based initiative.

10

THE MESSAGE OF THE FAITH-BASED initiative is that poverty persists because religious believers are not delivering social services. "Much of today's poverty has more to do with troubled lives than a troubled economy," Bush announced in 2001. The intelligent Christians at his side are surely less forgiving of economic forces, but unlike their predecessors they look the other way. The national debate on poverty has come down to this massive bid, as Bernard Zylstra candidly pronounced so long ago, to "disestablish secularism" in the social safety net.

Abraham Kuyper hated liberalism too, but he would have nothing to do with the current outpouring of "religious wisdom" on poverty, not so long as there was silence on the corrupting evil of hoarded wealth and its disintegrative influence in the political system. Gratuitous wealth and poverty, Kuyper said, are the marks of a society that "is losing touch with Christ" and "lies in the dust bowed down before Mammon." Since 2000, 4.3 million Americans have become poor by the federal definition, and the number living in extreme poverty (the extreme-poverty line is half as high as the poverty line) is now 15.3 million. In 2000, the top one hundredth of one percent of the income scale—a mere 13,400 households—had nearly as much income as *the entire 100 million people at the bottom.* These evils scripture makes plain.

The two most notable trends in American society today are religious revival and growing inequality. Remarkably, there is little discussion of why these trends might go hand in hand. Kuyper would not trust religion to say anything if it did not address this question from the start. He understood the ideological power of religion as well as its miraculous strength. In 1891, he delivered an address of lasting importance called "The Social Problem and the Christian Religion" at the opening of the first Christian Social Congress in the Netherlands. His watchword then is no less relevant now:

> Whenever one uses the phrase "social question," one recognizes, in the most general sense, that serious doubt has arisen about the *soundness of the social structure in which we live*. One thereby acknowledges that public opinion is at war over the foundation on

which a more appropriate—and therefore more livable—social order may be built. Merely to raise the question in no way implies that it has to be answered in a *socialistic* manner. The solution one reaches can be of a totally different kind. Only one thing is necessary if the social question is to exist for you: you must realize the untenability of the present state of affairs, and you must account for this untenability not by incidental causes but by a fault in the very foundation of our society's organization. If you do not acknowledge this and think that social evil can be exorcised through an increase in piety, or through friendlier treatment or more generous charity, then you may believe we face a religious question or possibly a philanthropic question, but you will not recognize the *social* question. This question does not exist for you until you exercise an architectonic critique of human society, which leads to the desire for a different arrangement of the social order.

"A different arrangement of the social order." To answer Kuyper's call, let us return to the Hebrew prophets that President Bush cites as his inspiration for the faith-based initiative. What is striking is their richly detailed understanding of how poverty is created and perpetuated in defiance of God's justice.

The prophets defended God's covenant with the people of Israel, who were brought out of slavery into a land of familial abundance and shared prosperity. God's laws embraced justice: they gave relief to the indebted, resources to those without property, freedom to the enslaved. For example, the poor must have access to interest-free loans (Exod. 22:25), and after seven years even the principal is to be forgiven: "The Lord's time for canceling debts has been proclaimed" (Deut. 15:1–11). The Jubilee

Year provisions of Leviticus 25 created an economic institution designed to maintain an equitable distribution of land—productive resources—among God's people. Every 50 years the land was to be restored to the control of kinship clans as originally provided, based on proportionate need, when Israel took possession of the land (Num. 26). The theological foundation of such a policy of permanent redistribution was simply that God was the land's only true owner. All God's people are equally guests on his land and therefore subject to his laws and to the objectives they are meant to sustain.

A consistent objective of the ancient covenant was to ensure basic sustenance for all the people and to prevent accumulations of land and power that would lead to deprivation and servitude. Thus, the laws of the covenant combined tithings earmarked for social welfare (Deut. 14:28–29) with redistributive policies such as Jubilee. Sustenance meant more than subsistence. In Hannah's prayer, God not only helps the poor but reverses their fortunes: "He raises the poor from the dust and lifts the needy from the ash heap; in order to give them a place with nobles, and have them inherit a throne of honor" (1 Sam. 2:8).

When the prophets arose against backsliding regimes, oppression of the poor was viewed as evidence of covenantal failure. Isaiah declares, "Woe to those who make unjust laws, to those who issue oppressive decrees, to deprive the poor of their rights and rob my oppressed people of justice, making widows their prey and robbing the fatherless" (10:1–2). Amos decries those who "trample on the heads of the poor as upon the dust of the ground and deny justice to the oppressed" (2:7). Micah castigates the legalized thievery of the wealthy rulers who devise new laws to subvert God's justice: "Woe to those who plan iniquity, to those who plot evil on their beds! At morning light they carry it out because it is in their power to do it. They covet fields and seize them, and houses, and take them. They defraud a man of his home, a fellowman of his inheritance" (2:1–2). It is no wonder the philosopher William Godwin said that "the doctrine of the injustice of accumulated property has been the foundation of all religious morality."

The timeless words of Psalm 73 describe how the wealthy and powerful turn the nation against God with false piety and seductive rhetoric. The petitioner tells of how he "almost lost his foothold" because he envied the "prosperity of the wicked":

They have no struggles; their bodies are healthy and strong. They are free from the burdens common to man; they are not plagued by human ills. Therefore pride is their necklace; they clothe themselves with violence. … Their mouths lay claim to heaven, and their tongues take possession of the earth. Therefore their people turn to them and drink up waters in abundance. They say, "How can God Know? Does the Most High have knowledge?" This is what the wicked are like—always carefree, they increase in wealth.

The New Testament extends these prophetic themes. The Letter of James warns of the woes awaiting those who have "hoarded wealth in the last days": "Look! The wages you failed to pay the workmen who mowed your fields cry out against you." In the Gospel of Mark, Jesus tells crowds gathered in

the Temple about a man who rented a vineyard to some farmers and then went away on
a journey. At harvest time, the owner sent
a servant to collect a portion of the fruit
from the tenants. But they beat the servant
and sent him away. A second servant they
struck on the head, and a third they killed.
Finally, the owner of the vineyard sent his
own son, but the tenants, seeing that he was
the heir to the vineyard, killed him to make
the inheritance theirs. "What then will the
owner of the vineyard do?" Jesus asked. "He
will come and kill those tenants and give the
vineyard to others." The covenantal theme
of God's ownership of the land is used here,
of course, to attack the economic injustices
of the Jerusalem elites and portend their violent overthrow. Only the crowds at Jesus'
side prevented the authorities from arresting
him on the spot, the Gospel tells us.

With a few exceptions in the wisdom literature, the Hebrew Bible is generally silent on the behavior or worthiness of the poor. So are the Gospels, although Matthew's claim that many social problems "come out of the heart" (15:19) is sometimes interpreted to mean that you can only change society "one heart at a time," not through broader efforts to establish justice. Clearly, however, the behavior and institutions of the rich and powerful are a major focus of prophetic biblical authority. While the ultimate suffering is corporate—exile and reenslavement of the nation—Israel's covenantal failure is laid again and again at the feet of the wealthy and powerful. In a contemporary light, it could be said the prophetic tradition does not blame the victim.

It is conceivable to put this in a comparative light and say that today there is no causal linkage between some people's wealth and others' deprivation: supply-side economists have been arguing this for decades. But as Irving Kristol wrote 30 years ago, resolving economic "tradeoffs," whatever the technical validity of such a notion, cannot be the basis of any lasting social consensus. People "cannot for long accept a society in which power, privilege, and property are not distributed according to some morally meaningful criteria." The biblical criteria of freedom from debt and servitude and access to resources are clear enough.

Direct care for the poor is required by Judeo-Christian faith. Feeding the hungry, sating the thirsty, sheltering the stranger, healing the sick—"Whatever you did for one of the least of these brothers of mine, you did for me," Jesus tells his disciples near the end of his life. But to anyone truly inspired by the Hebrew prophets and Jesus, the limits of this care, whether delivered by churches or not, should be disconcertingly clear. Jesus was not put on the cross for what he did to help the poor, but for what he preached against the rich and powerful. Hoarding wealth was gravely unjust, he taught in the parable of the vineyard. But as the prophets before him taught, the unmistakable defilement occurred when the wealthy tenants who hoarded God's fruits commended piety to everyone else. "For day after day they seek me out; they seem eager to know my ways, as if they were a nation that does what is right and has not forsaken the commands of its God" (Isa. 58:2).

It is certainly unorthodox for any war on poverty inspired by Hebrew prophecy to ignore the growing gap between rich and poor and wealth's dominion in our political system. The top one percent of households who own more than half of all the financial wealth in the country are not blameless from a prophetic point of view. But lavishing these people with even more wealth—nearly half a trillion dollars' worth of tax cuts between 2001 and 2010—radically defies what the prophets taught about upholding true religion. Yet this is what our president did after answering God's call in 2000. "I believe God wants me to be president," Bush told a group of religious leaders in 1999, on the day he was inaugurated for his second term as governor of Texas.

A nation so arrogant and so boastful of the religious favor apparently reflected in its extraordinary material wealth cannot allow poverty to persist or grow, decade after decade, without finally emptying itself of that favor—what believers call the grace of God.

This finally threatens the nation with moral exclusion from the civilized world, inviting tyranny to stay God's hand.

Ultimately, there is something to be said for the idea of giving scale to the kind of care that faith communities provide to those in need. But wealth and power conspire—that is the only word for it today—to undermine religious good works at every turn. And religious leaders do the bidding of wealth and power by making sure that even the simplest questions of justice can be safely ignored by those who benefit from injustice.

President Bush's commitment to religious autonomy as the cure for poverty cannot be reconciled with his administration's unwavering allegiance to the wealthiest Americans. But even if such autonomy were realized, the success of churches' efforts would rest on what they did with their freedom. Perhaps most churches would go on doing what they do best—helping their own middle-class members have more fulfilling middle-class lives. But institutions can and do change from within in response to social changes that threaten their beliefs and traditions. And the period we are now entering is certainly one that the prophets would have regarded as threatening. If a person can be born again from reading a psalm—as I saw happen once—why not a church that tries to apply scripture, and why not hundreds of churches or thousands, united together to do as the prophets did?

BIBLIOGRAPHIC NOTE

The most comprehensive study of the political history of the faith-based initiative is Amy E. Black, Douglas L. Koopman, and David K. Ryden's *Of Little Faith: The Politics of George W. Bush's Faith-Based Initiatives* (Washington, D.C.: Georgetown University Press, 2004). Based in part on interviews with key players, it carefully details and analyzes the failed legislative efforts to expand the faith-based initiative during Bush's first term. There is as yet no detailed study of the history of charitable-choice legislation, but *Of Little Faith* covers some of that earlier ground.

Bush's administrative strategy for the faith-based initiative is carefully documented in *The Expanding Administrative Presidency*, a study published in 2004 by the Roundtable on Religion and Social Welfare Policy (available at www.religionandsocialpolicy.org). The Roundtable also conducts a running series of studies on legal developments under charitable choice and the faith-based initiative, in addition to an extensive research program on the scope, scale, and effectiveness of religious social-service organizations. On the legal theory behind the faith-based initiative, an invaluable study is Stephen V. Monsma's *Positive Neutrality: Letting Religious Freedom Ring* (Grand Rapids: Baker Book House, 1995). The law-review literature on charitable choice and the faith-based initiative is immense, but a good overview is provided in the articles collected in *Welfare Reform & Faith-Based Organizations*, edited by Derek H. Davis and Barry Hankins (Waco, Tex.: J.M. Dawson Institute of Church–State Studies, 1999).

The best general source for understanding the theological background of the faith-based initiative is *Political Order and the Plural Structure of Society*, edited by James W. Skillen and Rockne M. McCarthy (Atlanta: Scholars Press, 1991). This study brings together primary theological sources on political order from the Catholic and Reformed traditions, along with commentary from a viewpoint of confessional rights within liberal democracy. A superb collection of Abraham Kuyper's writings is *Abraham Kuyper: A Centennial Reader*, edited by James D. Bratt (Grand Rapids: William B. Eerdmans Publishing Co., 1998). Kuyper's famous Stone Lectures, delivered at Princeton University in 1898, were recently reissued in Abraham Kuyper's *Lectures on Calvinism* (Grand Rapids: William B. Eerdmans Publishing Co., 2000). For Kuyper's powerful confessional viewpoint on the "social question," see *The Problem of Poverty*, edited by James W. Skillen (Grand Rapids: Baker Book House, 1991).

The last decade has seen a renaissance of Kuyper studies as his influence has grown among religious conservatives. Two important books on Kuyper's contemporary relevance are *Religion, Pluralism, and Public Life: Abraham Kuyper's Legacy for the Twenty-First Century*, edited by Luis E. Lugo (Grand Rapids: William B. Eerdmans Publishing Co., 2000), and John Bolt's *A Free Church, A Holy Nation: Abraham Kuyper's American Public Theology* (Grand Rapids: William B. Eerdmans Publishing Co., 2001).

Two essential early books by Harold Joseph Laski cover some of the same ground from an English pluralist perspective: *Studies in the Problem of Sovereignty* (Clark, N.J.: Lawbook Exchange, 2003; orig. publ. 1917) and *Authority in the Modern State* (Clark, N.J.: Lawbook Exchange, 2003; orig. publ. 1919). Also of great interest is Bernard Zylstra's penetrating study of Laski's thought, *From Pluralism to Collectivism* (Assen: Van Gorcum, 1968), unfortunately long out of print. For the Althusian background, see Daniel J.

Elazar's "Althusius and Federalism as Grand Design," (*Rechtstheorie* 14 [1997]: 209–218) and Andreas Føllesdal's "Survey Article: Subsidiarity" (*The Journal of Political Philosophy* 6, no. 2 [1998]: 190–218). A new edition of Althusius' extraordinary *Politica* is available from the Liberty Fund (www.libertyfund.org).

The Catholic theory of the state is not as well-defined as the Kuyperian model from a contemporary perspective. The classic study is Heinrich A. Rommen's *The State in Catholic Thought* (New York: Greenwood Press, 1969). Recent essays on subsidiarity from a conservative, anti-welfare-state perspective include Christopher Wolfe's "Subsidiarity: The 'Other' Ground of Limited Government" in *Catholicism, Liberalism, and Communitarianism: The Catholic Intellectual Tradition and the Moral Foundations of Democracy*, edited by Kenneth L. Grasso, Gerard V. Bradley, and Robert P. Hunt (Totowa, N.J.: Rowman & Littlefield Publishers, 1995). Some helpful commentary on subsidiarity is found in Charles E. Curran's *Catholic Social Teaching, 1891–present* (Washington, D.C.: Georgetown University Press, 2002). Robert K. Vischer investigates the links between subsidiarity, contemporary legal theory, and public policy in a groundbreaking law-review article, "Subsidiarity as a Principle of Governance: Beyond Devolution" (*Indiana Law Review* 35, no. 103 [2001]: 103–142).

Comparative political history helps to illuminate the faith-based initiative from a Christian Democratic perspective. By far the best study of Christian Democratic welfare systems is Kees van Kersbergen's *Social Capitalism: A Study of Christian Democracy and the Welfare State* (London: Routledge, 1995). Also valuable, from a range of national perspectives, is *European Christian Democracy: Historical Legacies and Comparative Perspectives*, edited by Thomas Kselman and Joseph A. Buttigieg (Notre Dame, Ind.: University of Notre Dame Press, 2003). Charles L. Glenn's excellent study, *The Ambiguous Embrace: Government and Faith-Based Schools and Social Agencies* (Princeton: Princeton University Press, 2000), combines historical and social-scientific analysis of religious pluralism in European education and welfare systems.

The earlier history of confessional conflict with liberal democracy, between the two world wars, is also very important for understanding the faith-based initiative. Good sources on this include *Political Catholicism in Europe, 1918–1965*, edited by Tom Buchanan and Martin Conway (Oxford: Oxford University Press, 1996); Edward Ross Dickinson's "Welfare, Democracy, and Fascism: The Political Crises in German Child Welfare, 1922–1933" (*German Studies Review* 22, no. 1 [1999]: 43–66); and especially Young-Sun Hong's *Welfare, Modernity, and the Weimar State, 1919–1933*

(Princeton: Princeton University Press, 1998). The connections between fascist and confessional attacks on welfare liberalism is a neglected area in political theory. On the corporatist dimension, see Peter J. Williamson's *Varieties of Corporatism: A Conceptual Discussion* (Cambridge, U.K.: Cambridge University Press, 1985).

BOSTON REVIEW BOOKS

Boston Review books are accessible, short books that take ideas seriously. They are animated by hope, committed to equality, and convinced that the imagination eludes political categories. The editors aim to establish a public space in which people can loosen the hold of conventional preconceptions and start to reason together across the lines others are so busily drawing.

THE END OF THE WILD   Stephen M. Meyer

GOD AND THE WELFARE STATE   Lew Daly